Preparing to Celebrate in Schools

Margaret Bick

NOVALIS

THE LITURGICAL PRESS

EJ DWYER

Design: Eye-to-Eye Design, Toronto

Layout: Suzanne Latourelle

Illustrations: Eugene Kral

Series Editor: Bernadette Gasslein

Business Office: Novalis, 49 Front Street East, 2nd floor, Toronto, Ontario M5E 1B3

Novalis: ISBN 2 89088 799 5

The Liturgical Press: ISBN 0-8146-2481-2
A Liturgical Press Book
Published in the United States of America by The Liturgical Press, Collegeville, Minnesota 56321

EJ Dwyer: ISBN 0-85574-055-8
EJ Dwyer, Locked Bag 71, Alexandria, NSW 2015, Australia

Reprint 2002

Printed in Canada.

Canadian Cataloguing in Publication Data

Bick, Margaret, 1948-
     Preparing to celebrate in schools

(Preparing for liturgy)
Includes bibliographical references.
ISBN 2-89088-799-5

     1. Worship (Religious education) 2. Catholic Church—Liturgy. 3. Catholic Church—Education. I. Title. II. Series.

We acknowledge the financial support of the Government of Canada through the Book Publishing Industry Development Program (BPIDP) for our publishing activities.

BX2045.C55B53 1997 264'.02'0083 C96-900847-3

Contents

Introduction

If you've picked up this little book, then you can probably, without pause, recite a handful of problems entailed in preparing to celebrate in schools. People problems, place problems, time problems, music problems, theme problems! Problems abound when we transplant the liturgy into this new, some would even say, foreign, environment.

Yet, school celebrations can be the source of much joy and spiritual enrichment for all concerned. Experience has shown that, when a strong program of liturgical formation is in place in the school, behaviour is seldom a problem in liturgy, and pastors, teachers and students all look forward to these opportunities to celebrate together. Amazingly, such a program can be put into place without any great disruption of the regular school program. This little book is designed to help you to carry out such a program in your situation.

Music in Catholic Worship, a document of the American bishops, explains why so much attention is given to how we celebrate: "Good celebrations foster and nourish faith. Poor celebrations may weaken and destroy it" (#6). Often we approach our liturgical problems with gimmicks and add-ons that simply create new problems and muddy the liturgical waters even more. But in fact, the cure is most often found, not in novelty rituals or other new inventions, but in the simplicity that arises from a fuller understanding and usage of the church's already rich storehouse of ritual possibilities. *Preparing to Celebrate in Schools* addresses the usual problems at their source. In this way it helps you both to avoid the worst in school liturgy and to build toward a strong program of liturgical formation in the school—a program which will lead to full, conscious and active participation by the students in the liturgical life of the church.

The *Directory for Masses with Children (DMC)*, an official liturgical document promulgated in 1973, addressed several fundamental issues in celebrating with children. It is required reading for all who celebrate with children in a school setting. If you don't have a copy, you should take time now—right now—to find one. (You can order it from the Canadian Conference of Catholic Bishops, Publications Service, 90 Parent Ave, Ottawa, ON K1N 7B1.) I'll be referring you to it repeatedly; it may be wise to mark important paragraphs in your copy of the document. Don't let the word 'children' in the title turn you away just because you work with older students. Good liturgy is good liturgy regardless of the age of the participants. You'll find that the liturgical and pastoral principles underlying the document apply to believers of all ages.

Ready? Let's begin!

Discussion Questions

1. What are the problems in your school celebrations right now?

2. What are the joys? What is working well?

3. Has there been a pattern of growth and improvement or is the quality of celebration declining? Outline what has happened.

4. Is there a copy of the *Directory for Masses with Children* available for use by those preparing school liturgy?

CHAPTER 1

What Are We Celebrating?

First Things First

The question in the title of this chapter is, by far, the single most important consideration for any liturgy planner. The life of a school community is packed with occasions that we can celebrate: unit themes, birthdays, new beginnings and welcomings, endings and good-byes, graduations, retirements; and special times such as Thanksgiving, Remembrance Day, Advent, Holy Week and the feasts of parish and school patrons.

If we fail to ask at the outset, "What are we celebrating?" we risk treating the liturgy like Jonathan Winters' coat-hanger. Winters, an American comedian, is famous for his routine which outlines the many uses for a simple metal coat-hanger. Hanging up clothing was never on his list! We Catholics tend to do the same with our liturgy. We use it for teaching, consciousness-raising and fund-raising. We use it for graduations, retirements and good-byes. We even use it as a kind of punctuation to begin or end our Catholic gatherings.

Each time we use the liturgy for a purpose for which it was never intended, we actually empty it of meaning and diminish its value. We tend to celebrate eucharist so often that it becomes commonplace, boring, tedious. The phrase 'celebration of eucharist' becomes a contradiction in terms. In addition, if we ask the liturgy to do things which, in reality, are beyond its scope, it should not surprise us when we run into difficulties, or when the results of all our preparations are less than satisfying.

Our Liturgy Has Only One 'Theme'

To understand what the celebration of eucharist is all about, we must look to the very heart of the celebration itself, the eucharistic prayer. Its opening dialogue distinctly reveals that this is a celebration of praise and thanks.

> *"Lift up your hearts."*
>
> *"We lift them up to the Lord."*
>
> *"Let us give thanks to the Lord our God."*
>
> *"It is right to give our thanks and praise."*

The prefaces clearly indicate that our praise and thanks are directed to God, whom we know as Trinity, for the work of creation and for all of God's marvellous deeds on behalf of humanity.

> *"God our Father,*
>
> *you have brought us here together*
>
> *so that we can give you thanks and praise*
>
> *for all the wonderful things you have done."*
>
> **(Eucharistic Prayer for Children I)**

Inevitably, the eucharistic prayer turns to praise and thanks for our salvation in Christ: for his gift of himself in life and death, for his passage through death to new life and Spirit-filled glory, and for our sharing in that new, glorified life. This mystery of our salvation in Christ is called 'the paschal mystery.'

> *"God our Father,*
>
> *we remember with joy*
>
> *all that Jesus did to save us.*
>
> *In this holy sacrifice,*
>
> *which he gave as a gift to his Church,*
>
> *we remember his death and resurrection."*
>
> **(Eucharistic Prayer for Children III)**

Even celebrations of reconciliation are oriented to the paschal mystery. By Christ's passage our salvation is won; by his passage our sins are forgiven.

"God the Father of all mercies,

by the death and resurrection of his Son

has reconciled the world to himself

and sent the Holy Spirit among us

for the forgiveness of sins;

through the ministry of the Church

may God grant you pardon and peace . . . "

(Absolution Prayer, Rite of Penance)

Every liturgical celebration is a celebration in the true and common sense of the word. As an occasion of thanks and praise, it should be festive and joyful. Penitential services celebrate the greatness of God's forgiveness; prayer services in time of great distress (war, natural disaster, other tragic happenings) celebrate the God whom we can always trust to hear our cries of pain and petition.

This challenges those preparing celebrations in schools to ask ourselves if we are expecting the eucharist to celebrate something it was never intended to celebrate. If we are having trouble finding an appropriate reading, if it seems that the eucharistic prayer is 'out of sync' with our intent for this gathering, or if we need to add parts to make the liturgy fit our intentions, we have good indicators that eucharist is not appropriate, or not the best option for this occasion.

There is no other theme for liturgical gatherings but the paschal mystery. At various points in the liturgical year we look at this mystery from different angles or emphasize certain aspects of it, but God and the paschal mystery are always at the centre of liturgical celebrations. We can highlight specific reasons to praise God in a celebration, but these reasons should not overshadow the central mystery of our faith proclaimed in the songs and prayers of the celebration.

Other Types of Celebration Are Possible

This brings us to the possibility of other kinds of celebrations. Too often, our actions and attitudes indicate a belief that eucharist is the only way Catholics can pray together. If we do not celebrate eucharist, many come away dissatisfied, as if such prayer is without value, or is unworthy of bearing Christ's presence. We forget Christ's promise: "Where two or three are gathered in my name, I am there among them" (Matthew 18:20). What are our options for celebration other than eucharist? Certainly the most common would be a celebration of the word. Others would include morning or evening prayer and traditional devotional exercises (rosary, Angelus, stations of the cross).

A celebration of the word is precisely what the name suggests. It is a festive occasion in which those who are present celebrate the good news of the kingdom of God, which we receive through Christ who is present and speaks in the word proclaimed. Usually such a celebration follows the same format as the liturgy of the word at mass: a greeting and opening prayer, readings, responsorial psalm, gospel acclamation and procession, homily, profession of faith and general intercessions. It should include joyful songs of praise and other sensually appealing indicators of our esteem for God's word: incense, candles, processions, gestures of honour. These celebrations are essential for the formation of younger students who are not yet allowed to share in the eucharistic meal.

The morning and evening prayer of the church's liturgy of the hours can be adapted for school settings. Such celebrations include the singing of praise in the psalms, a scripture reading and sung gospel canticle, and prayers on behalf of the world. For more information about celebrating morning and evening prayer, see *Preparing Morning and Evening Prayer* in this series.

Devotions usually have their own traditional structure. The *Constitution on the Sacred Liturgy* requires that these always be conducted in harmony with the liturgy, but not during the liturgy. This means celebrating them in the appropriate seasons of the liturgical year, in accordance with the spirit of the liturgy which is above all else joyful and oriented to the praise of God. They must be rooted in shared life, and characterized by the full, conscious and active participation of all present.

Celebrating the Saints

You may ask, "If liturgy is always directed to the Trinity, where do celebrations of Mary and other saints fit in?" Once again the liturgical texts for these occasions provide a key. If we look at the collect prayers of the mass, we note that, on Marian feasts and saints' days, prayer is still addressed to God for the gifts given to the church through these particular persons. We do not have masses *to* Mary or *to* other saints; rather we give thanks and praise for the work they accomplished and for the role models their lives and work provide to a struggling church.

Celebrating saints—especially the feasts of parish and school patrons on their particular feast day—is appropriate in schools. But we must plan from a balanced perspective, and with the church's priority of feasts in mind. For example, if we can celebrate eucharist only once during the fifty days of the Easter season, then it is best to respect and celebrate the Easter season, rather than honouring Mary or another saint, or picking some other theme. Mary and the saints can be honoured in other kinds of celebrations. The *Born of the Spirit Series* (Canadian Conference of Catholic Bishops) follows the advice of Pope Paul VI's encyclical, *Marialis Cultis*, placing Mary in the rich context of the Advent season, where we honour her and model ourselves on her as God-bearer and faithful servant. School liturgy planners do well to follow the lead of the catechetical materials.

Why Celebrate in School?

This important question goes to the heart of how we will approach the task of preparing to celebrate. First, it is important to understand that celebration is more a learning experience than a test situation. (It is, of course, above all an act of worship, an encounter with God!) Any problems we encounter should be treated as indicators for the direction of future formation rather than as commentaries on the students' faith or on the school's program in religious education.

But if we speak of it as a learning situation, it is in a very particular way. One of the important functions of liturgical celebration is to form us in the faith of the church, to help us to know our God in a way that lessons and classroom work can never match. The signs and rituals we use in the liturgy speak to us at a profound level. And so we find the key to our reason for celebrating in the school setting in paragraph 21 of the *DMC*. "It is always to be kept in mind that these eucharistic celebrations must lead children toward the celebration of Mass with adults, especially the Masses at which the Christian community must come together on Sundays." Whatever we do with students in school celebrations will affect their participation in parish liturgy. It may lead them naturally to it. But it could create a desire for novelty which has never been a part of our liturgy. It could create other expectations that the parish liturgy can never meet, or train them in habits they will have to unlearn to participate in parish liturgy. School and parish celebrations must work hand in hand towards the liturgical formation of our students.

In Summary

1. Every liturgical celebration is primarily a celebration of the paschal mystery.

2. Other forms of celebration are possible, but must always remain in harmony with the church's faith and liturgy. These include celebrations of the word, morning and evening prayer, and devotions.

3. We may honour the saints in our celebrations and ask them to pray with and for us, but liturgy is always directed to God.

4. Our school celebrations will either facilitate or impede the children's full participation in liturgy with adults, especially at the Sunday eucharist. School celebrations are intended to lead students to participation in the parish celebration.

Discussion Questions

1. List all the school celebrations of the past year.

2. Consider these questions about the celebrations you have listed:

   a) Which ones included liturgical elements?
   Was liturgical celebration appropriate on these occasions? What other options could have been exercised?

   b) Was each celebration in harmony with its moment in the liturgical year?

   c) What made each a festive occasion?

CHAPTER 2

How We Celebrate Is Who We Are

Special occasions give us cause to ponder how things came to be. Family reunions, weddings and funerals lead us to ponder our family habits, the ways in which our families celebrate themselves and how we pass on this family ethos to the next generation. We do not sit our children down and lecture them about the flow of the day of a wedding or a funeral. Instead, on each occasion, we bring them along, and allow them to grow into the family pattern at their own speed. From the example of the loving adults who surround them on such occasions and answer their questions, our children begin to know that in this family we honour our dead by touching their hand while uttering a short (very short!) prayer. And we honour the newly-weds by clinking our glasses with our knives when it's been too long since they kissed. And on it goes. Other families may do things in other ways, but we do them thus and so because we are the Rigafratz family of Lower North Crook. It's a matter of who we are. And doing it right together makes us who we are. This is a major theme of the story *Fiddler on the Roof*. Like Tevye, we know that, when we bend tradition beyond its limit, we risk our identity, our very existence.

We All Need Liturgical Formation

So it is with our church family. How we celebrate is part of who we are. Therefore, we must celebrate properly to be ourselves, to remember properly who we are. Because liturgy is patterned and repetitive, it can form us. Each time we follow the pattern, the pattern becomes a part of us. For better or worse, the patterns of our celebrations become part of us, part of our faith, part of our way of being in the world. Thus how we celebrate matters. Our way of celebrating should either affirm or challenge our way of being in the world. It forces us to ask ourselves, "How can I behave in this way when I worship in that way?"

Because liturgy does its work of formation at such a profound level, we who take a leadership role in school celebrations need to do our work with the fullest possible awareness of what liturgy is all about. This means that school staffs need to be involved in a process of liturgical formation as much as the students do. Administrators at both board-wide and local school levels should ensure that opportunities for liturgical education are offered at least annually to school staff members. And those who prepare liturgical celebrations for teacher groups should ensure that all celebrations model the best liturgical principles.

Students, like teachers, also will need two kinds of liturgical formation: formation which happens in a structured educational setting and formation which comes from the experience of celebration. Although formation has often been attempted in a so-called 'teaching mass,' where everything is explained as the celebration progresses, teaching and celebration do not mix. Don't do it! The process of celebration is at its formative best when it happens in three distinct and separate stages: preparation, celebration and reflection.

Preparation As Formation

Students need to be involved in two kinds of preparation: of the celebration and of themselves. To the extent possible, students can help to decide which of the many options within the liturgical pattern will be used—songs, readings, decor and the arrangement of furniture, intentions for general intercessions, even who is best to perform each ministry. The teacher may have to present younger children with a short list of possibilities from which they may choose; older students with more experience may be able to assemble their own list of suggestions.

Time for adequate preparation is important (*DMC #27*). The better prepared students are to celebrate, the better disposed they will be. Adequate preparation means that every student knows all the songs that will be used. Adequate preparation means that every person present is very familiar with the readings that will be proclaimed. Persons with special tasks to perform are well-rehearsed and comfortable with their assignments. Any new gesture which may be unfamiliar or any gestures which have proven problematic at past celebrations are rehearsed by all well in advance of the celebration. Regularly scheduled mass practices are a part of any good program of liturgical formation. The energy we put into preparation indicates of the importance of the celebration.

Celebration As Formation

Celebration forms us just as surely as the hands of the potter form the clay. Angry, embittered hands produce angry, bitter pieces. Patient, peaceful hands produce something serene. So it is with liturgy. Boring liturgy not only bores us for the moment, but, over time, it forms us into boring Catholics who believe religion and boredom go hand-in-hand. Lively, life-giving liturgy forms us into Catholics who draw their life from their worship, their faith, their God; they go out to give life to the world as well. We do not leave liturgy untouched.

Celebrations teach us how to celebrate, and they also teach us how to live, how to be in the world. They teach us about the kingdom and how to live it now. The festive music of our liturgy teaches us the joyous nature of our worship and our faith. But it also trains us in the habits of joyful living. The sign of peace teaches us that peace is a prerequisite for celebration and for kingdom life, while it trains us in the art of reaching out in reconciliation and forgiveness in daily life.

If we wish our students to grow into the church's liturgy, then it is imperative to use the church's language of celebration and to assist them in becoming fluent in it when we celebrate with them. Ritual is the church's language of celebration. And children have an innate ritual capacity. They engage constantly and comfortably in symbolic play. All we have to do is to give them adequate exposure to and experience with our ritual language, and they will begin to explore it, manipulate it, appreciate it and feel at home with it. How can we tell if it's working? Children who experience rich, colourful, dignified processions will play procession at home using empty wrapping paper tubes for candles and a beach towel for vestments. And don't young children love to play communion using Ritz crackers or even loonies? Why not have a 'church centre' or 'mass centre' or a 'legoland church' in primary classrooms? What a natural way for the children to explore their place in the church!

But, of course, they also need opportunities to participate fully in the real thing. So, in schools we must take every opportunity to explore the church's use of symbol and ritual in our celebrations. We have a rich treasury on which to draw. This includes substances and objects (water, scented oil, food and drink, candle, cross, Bible, table, incense, ashes), gestures (sign of the cross/blessing, signing self or another with a cross using thumb, laying on one or both hands, sharing food, sign of peace, sprinkling with water), and postures (standing, uplifted hands, procession, bowing, genuflecting, kneeling). These can be combined in many ways for use in non-eucharistic celebrations. Here are some examples of ritual gestures: signing one's own or another's forehead, lighting a candle from a main candle, laying a hand on a Bible or lectionary, placing a grain of incense on coals, standing to pray or sing, joining in a procession with Bible, cross, or candle.

These ritual actions may be accompanied by appropriate phrases from the liturgy or from scripture, spoken by a minister or by each individual, or they may be carried out in silence. Here is an example: students pass a candle to one another around a circle saying, "Keep the flame of faith alive in your heart" (text from the *Rite of Baptism*).

Such rituals are most useful in celebrations of the word. In addition to introducing students to the church's ritual vocabulary, including such ritual actions helps students to embody their prayer, to feel personally involved in the celebration and to internalize its meaning.

Reflection As Formation

Notice that meaning was not mentioned as a prominent factor in preparation or celebration. We do not need to tell students what the gestures will mean; this is the job of the gestures themselves. Symbols are to be experienced, not explained. Discussion of meaning is reserved for after the celebration. Every student who attended must be led through a reflection on what happened at the celebration. (Notice that this is a key element in the approach to celebration in the *Born of the Spirit Series* published by the Canadian Conference of Catholic Bishops.) Invite students to recall their favourite moments; help them find meaning in these and other moments in the ritual. In this process of reflection, we determine what meaning the students actually gleaned from the gestures and signs as they happened, we validate their experience and then relate their experience of the rituals to how the church interprets them.

Another important aspect of this post-celebration reflection is discussing the uncomfortable moments: "I couldn't see Father." "She pinched me." "He kept fooling around." "I forgot what to do." These comments often provide direction for future liturgical adaptation (e.g., rearranging the space and seating plan) and the school's efforts in the liturgical formation of the students (e.g., practising the sign of peace).

In Summary

1. Celebration is a powerful tool for forming students in their Christian identity.

2. Staff and students alike need liturgical formation.

3. Each celebration has three phases, each of which plays a role in formation: preparation, celebration and reflection.

4. Ritual is the language of our liturgy and children have an innate ritual capacity.

Discussion Questions

1. What traditions are part of your family's celebrations? How did you learn them? How are you passing them on?

2. To what extent has your school staff been offered opportunities in liturgical formation and education?

3. To what extent have you involved students in preparation, reflection and evaluation of school celebrations? How could such involvement be enhanced?

4. Which items of the church's ritual vocabulary have been used in your school celebrations? Which could most easily be introduced into the school repertoire?

CHAPTER 3

When Should We Celebrate?

Celebrating, rejoicing, and praising God are essential character-istics of Christian life. St. Paul urges us to "rejoice always, pray without ceasing, give thanks in all circumstances; for this is the will of God in Christ Jesus for you" (1 Thessalonians 5:23). Every school day brings with it new reasons to celebrate. For this reason, prayer is built into the timetable every day. Our larger celebrations build on these daily prayer experiences. How should we schedule these larger celebrations? This question leads us in two directions. In considering the timing of our school celebrations, we must respect the needs of both the student, and of the liturgy and the liturgical year. First, let's deal with the students' needs.

The Right Time for the Students

Liturgical documents often talk about the importance of the person's disposition or ability to fruitfully enter into the celebration (*DMC* #26). For most people, but especially for young children, time is a significant factor in their disposition. Many schools still operate on a "first Friday of the month" mass schedule. However, this does not take into account the needs of students. Choosing a time and day which, for this group of students, is most conducive to religious celebration is essential to the success of the celebration. (The day before Christmas vacation and the Friday of the first week of school are inappropriate times for celebration for most children.) When those preparing celebrations give serious consideration to receptivity of the students in scheduling celebrations, discipline problems are reduced, and later reflection and mystagogy is more fruitful.

An adequate period of preparation is also a critical factor in scheduling celebrations. The *DMC* insists that our schedules take preparation time into consideration (#27). It is crucial to establish the celebration schedule early in the school year.

The Right Time for the Liturgy

Now we move to the demands of the liturgy. Time has always been an important factor in Christian celebration. Of all the days of the week, Sunday is the Lord's Day, the day the community must gather for eucharist. Of all the hours of every day, the community is called to pray morning and evening. We have festive seasons and seasons that prepare for them. And occasionally we have individual, specific dates, and even specific hours on those days, which call for celebration. It is precisely because these times carry so much meaning that we must respect them.

When many families do not participate in parish life or when parish celebrations are in some way deficient, school liturgy planners are often tempted to use school celebrations as replacements for parish celebrations. But we do children no favour when we give in to such temptations. The job of school liturgy is to lead children to full participation in the community's liturgy, not to replace it. The school can no more substitute for the parish than the parish can substitute for the school. And celebrating out of time simply teaches children that time is irrelevant and all that matters is that the thing gets done.

Christmas and the days between Palm Sunday and Easter are those most frequently violated in this manner. December celebrations must be Advent—not Christmas—liturgies. Usually a few days of the Christmas season remain when we return to school in January; we do well to celebrate these with appropriate festivity. Again, the *Born of the Spirit Series* provides a healthy example of how this can be done.

Palm Sunday is not to be repeated at a school mass. Nor should we jump the gun on the Holy Thursday and Good Friday liturgies. Instead, assuming that students will participate in parish liturgies, we should schedule school celebrations that prepare students to participate in the community's liturgy.

In addition, we must ensure that school festivities during the preparatory seasons of Advent and Lent are balanced by our observation of the festive seasons themselves, Christmas-Epiphany and the fifty days of the Easter season. For more detailed information on the church's year, see *Preparing the Liturgical Year* in this series.

The Right Time for Something Else

One of the most frequent requests I receive is to suggest readings for 'theme' masses—friendship and the environment are among the most popular. By the time people come to me it's too late for them to switch to a non-liturgical format. But I do hint at the source of the problem by pointing out that, although these themes are honourable and not at odds with the gospel, they are not the focus of Jesus' preaching. The gospel, in fact, calls us to grow beyond our circles of friendship toward love for all humanity; it focuses more directly on the call to care for all humanity than on care for the environment. We praise and thank God for the gifts of friendship and creation within the liturgy, but it is quite difficult to fit these themes under the umbrella of the good news of salvation and paschal mystery, the proper focus of the eucharistic celebration. The bottom line is this: these themes are perfect occasions for something else—perhaps a prayer service with some liturgical elements, e.g., a sign of peace, or a blessing.

In Summary

1. Always keep in mind the nature and needs of the students when scheduling celebrations.

2. School liturgies supplement parish liturgy; they cannot replace it, no matter how good our intention may be.

3. All school celebrations must harmonize with the liturgy and the liturgical year.

4. Eucharist is not always the best way to integrate our faith into the school program.

Discussion Questions

1. Considering the nature and needs of your students, what would be the most appropriate time during the school week for you and your students to celebrate?

2. How much time would your students need to adequately prepare for a celebration?

3. What moments in the liturgical year should be celebrated at the school? How can they be celebrated without appearing to replace the parish celebration?

CHAPTER 4

What's a Great Liturgy Doing in a Place Like This?

Our liturgy, like water, is shaped by its container. The place we use for worship can restrict us or overwhelm us. It can keep us apart or bring us into community. Just like the human ministers of the liturgy, the worship space either serves the liturgy or impedes it. It is never neutral. So, the space we use and the way we use it are important. But the space we use for worship is not just a container, it is an active minister in the liturgy. It has sign value, it communicates meaning. Its general design makes a statement about what we believe to be important and what is not. For more detailed information on liturgical space, see also *Preparing the Environment for Worship* in this series.

Finding Appropriate Space

Space can be problematic in school celebrations—classrooms, gymnasiums, and libraries were not designed with the principles of good liturgy in mind. Bringing students into an over-sized, inflexible church building presents a different, but equally challenging, set of problems. Needless, to say, the parish church, when it is appropriate to the group, is the preferable space for worship. The church building has been set aside for liturgical use; it is, in fact, the *domus ecclesiae*, the home of the church. Furthermore, using the parish church helps to strengthen the bond between the students and their parish, and frequent visits help them feel at home there. But the *DMC* mandates us to choose carefully a space within the church that allows children to feel at ease as they should in a living liturgy. If you cannot find such a space within the parish church, the *DMC* recommends using another worthy space outside the church (#25).

Ideally, of course, each school would have a space set aside for celebration. With a bit of imagination, an empty classroom can be converted into a chapel. In this case, it is advisable to restrain your imagination! Leave the space flexible enough so that it can house many kinds of celebration and allow each celebration to have its own character.

Size Is Important

What do we look for in a worship space? First, the size of the space should be appropriate to the size of group—to both the physical size of the individuals and the number of individuals in the group. We can expect squirming when the feet of children seated in church pews don't touch the ground. And children packed together on mats on the gym floor are not easily disposed to raise their minds and hearts to God.

Here are some ideas for adapting spaces that are less than ideal. Use and decorate movable dividers to shrink a room that is too big for the group. This can even be done in a parish church. Invest in one or more area rugs to cover a gym floor or classroom floor when the group gathers for liturgy. Reserve them for liturgical use. In a church building, gather students on the floor near the lectern for the liturgy of the word and make a procession to surround the altar for the liturgy of the eucharist.

And remember: there is great wisdom in the *DMC*'s observation that full, conscious and active participation by students is inhibited when the number of children who celebrate is very great (#28). Smaller group liturgies should be far more frequent than whole school celebrations.

A Worthy Space

Next, the space must have an inherent air of dignity and beauty. In the absence of a school chapel, a neat, well-organized classroom, a clean gymnasium with large and small equipment removed or well-hidden, a library with the clutter and rotating book stands out of sight and out of reach can all be starting points for creating an adequate worship space. But, of course, these are only starting points. We also need markers, not felt markers, but items used to signal that something special is about to happen. Markers can be effective only if they are an instantly recognizable part of a predictable pattern. Therefore they must be used repeatedly and consistently. The special area rug reserved for liturgy, the special rearrangement of the furniture, meditative music played beforehand on a good sound system ("Hey! It sounds like church!"), the scent of a beeswax candle burning ("Hey! It smells like church!"), a large cross and/or banner at the doorway: these are but a few possible markers.

A Space for the Church's Banquet

When arranging a space for liturgy we are tempted to model the layout on the parish church. Often, however, most of these buildings were not designed for post-Vatican II liturgy; in copying their design we also inherit their built-in problems. Older churches are modelled on the theatre, where the special ministers are the active performers or celebrants and other worshippers are the passive audience whose attention focuses on the action in the sanctuary. Contemporary liturgy is modelled on the festive family meal, where the household of God gathers around the banquet table of the kingdom. The gathering certainly has focal points, but the assembly is aware that everyone celebrates. Everyone present has a necessary role in the celebration; all praise God together.

In addition, because the *DMC* encourages us to involve students in gesture and processions, the space must allow for this (#33). For seating, choose appropriately-sized chairs, floor cush-

ions or carpeting with the needs of the students in mind. Remember: the younger the students are, the closer they must be to the focal points to feel that they are part of the action.

Preparing the Space

Involve some of the students who will be worshipping in preparing the place—decorating, arranging furniture, setting the table (#29). You can display children's art in a dignified arrangement (#36). Students can be involved in creating banners which can be used as markers and tone-setters. If several smaller groups are coming together for liturgy, each group can design and contribute a square to a quilt-like banner. The creation of the banner square can help to focus the group's preparatory activities. With the help of Velcro strips or a sewing machine, assemble the squares; dedicate the banner at a brief prayer service *before* the celebration. Involving students in arranging the worship space can enhance their awareness of liturgical colours and the various objects and "stuff" we use for liturgy: cloths, candles, books, dishes, etc. Their work in preparing the place helps them to feel at home in the liturgy and is itself a form of active participation.

In Summary

1. Space is important because it can restrict or enhance what we do in liturgy and it makes a statement about our faith.

2. To become adequate worship spaces, school spaces will need adaptations of various kinds.

3. Schools can create markers which delineate and designate sacred space.

4. The space should reflect the fact that our liturgy is modelled on a great banquet.

5. Preparing the space is active involvement in the liturgy.

Discussion Questions

1. What are the good points of the space you now use for school celebrations? What are the problems? Brainstorm to come up with possible solutions or coping strategies, or even alternative spaces.

2. What markers do you now use to delineate or designate sacred space? If none, how can you create some?

3. To what extent are students now involved in preparing the space for celebration?

4. Is a chapel a possibility for your school?

CHAPTER 5

How Can We Keep From Singing?

Think about it! The entrance hymn, Lord, Have Mercy, Glory to God, psalm, gospel acclamation, general intercessions, Holy, Holy, memorial acclamation, Great Amen, Lamb of God, communion hymn: all these musical pieces should be recited only under the same circumstances in which we would recite, rather than sing, "Happy Birthday!" (That's why it feels so funny reciting them!) Everyone knows and sings "Happy Birthday" regardless of the quality of their singing voice or the availability of accompaniment and leadership. Such should be our familiarity with and attitude towards the music of our liturgy, especially in celebrations with children. Students should be able to participate in the music of the liturgy without song sheets or overhead projectors. Only then are they truly celebrating. Too often these worship 'aids' become simply another reading task which distracts from the spirit of celebration.

The Ministry of Music

Music is one of the strongest formative influences in the liturgy. Human society has long recognized the power of music to reach into the depth of our being and to bond people together. The music of our liturgy carries the truths of our faith to the core of our being. Joining our voices in liturgical song can, like the rousing chorus of a national anthem or even a drinking song, create instant camaraderie and unity. If we want the truth of the music to reach every heart, if we want every heart to be lifted in God's praise, if we want all these voices to be joined as one, then we will do everything in our power to make sure that we enable every voice to sing.

Some Musical Priorities

Music is the one element in the liturgy where we are allowed the greatest freedom of choice. The power of the music compels us to choose carefully. One of the most important tasks of those who are planning the program of liturgical formation in the school is building a musical repertoire. First, list all the liturgical music the students know well. Sort the list into groups according to the part of the mass for which it is appropriate. (For help in this work, see *Preparing Music for Celebration* in this series.)

Priority 1: If your list does not include any acclamations for the eucharistic prayers for masses with children, give these priority as the next additions to the repertoire. (With older students, learn the eucharistic acclamations and other acclamations and litanies that are used in the parish Sunday celebration.) Other gaps should be filled according to the following priorities:

Priority 2: psalm and gospel acclamation. Use seasonal psalms which may be used year after year, use an engaging setting of the gospel acclamation which may be prolonged to allow a procession through the assembly with the book; the gospel acclamation must be omitted if it is not sung.

Priority 3: songs for the entrance procession and communion procession. Use pieces with short verses and a lively refrain to facilitate participation—psalms are a good choice.

Priority 4: Lord, Have Mercy (a litany; note the patterned repetitive response), general intercessions (yes, they should be sung! it makes another litany), Lamb of God (a litany to accompany the breaking of the bread and pouring of consecrated wine).

Give Students a Voice

Careful development of the school's liturgical repertoire is essential to enhancing student participation in school celebrations. Students will give up trying to learn new songs for liturgy if new songs come too frequently or are never used again. Planning the repertoire ensures that music will be used often enough for comfort, while allowing for the growth that will lend variety when necessary. The parish repertoire can be a source for new liturgical music in the school. Consultation with parish musicians should be part of the long-range planning process. Experience has shown that, when this is done carefully, participation in parish liturgy improves. Is this not the goal of our work?

Certainly, you will need some pieces which are written especially for use in celebrations with children. But be aware that not all religious music is liturgical music. People tend to label as 'religious' any piece that mentions a religious personage or expresses a sentiment which is in harmony with the gospel message. But the use of the term 'liturgical music' requires us to narrow the field considerably. Liturgical music is music that meets the rather stringent requirements of the liturgy in general and of the particular part of the liturgy in which it is to be used. These requirements are outlined in the *National Bulletin on Liturgy* #72, "Music in Our Liturgy," in *Preparing Music for Celebration* in this series and in the American documents, *Music in Catholic Worship* and *Liturgical Music Today*. Not even all the pieces in the *Catholic Book of Worship* are included for use in the celebration of eucharist. Be sure to consult one of the documents listed above for guidance. A good example of liturgical music for children is the music composed for the 1995 version of *We Belong to the Lord Jesus*, the Year 2 program of the *Born of the Spirit Series* of the CCCB.

For Those Who Preside

Never underestimate your role as a minister of music! Experience has shown that the assembly's singing increases when the priest also sings, no matter what other kind of musical leadership there is. You do not have to lead. You don't even have to be heard. (You shouldn't be heard over the voice of the assembly!) Just make it obvious that you are singing. If you are not singing, one or more of the following is likely to occur:

1. Students will assume singing is not important.

2. Students will assume singing is optional.

3. Students will assume this is a performance for the priest, not communal worship.

4. Students will assume singing at liturgy is just for kids.

All this goes for the other adults present, too!

In Summary

1. Music is an integral part of the liturgy, not an add-on or a frill.

2. Music has the power to carry meaning deep within the person and to create a bond of unity within the liturgical assembly.

3. We should decide what parts we will sing according to established priorities. Every liturgy planning group should have a list of the school's liturgical repertoire. And remember: not all religious music is liturgical music.

4. Singing is for everyone.

Discussion Questions

1. How would you rate student participation in singing at school celebrations?

2. What factors are enhancing singing? What is getting in the way? (Ask the students, too.)

3. Who will be responsible for establishing and directing the growth of the school's liturgical repertoire?

CHAPTER 6

The *Directory for Masses with Children* - Definitely Not the Yellow Pages!

We are accustomed to think of a directory as a list of names with corresponding addresses and phone numbers. But there is a second, less familiar meaning used in the church setting. It refers to a document which contains a set of directions for the application of general law in specific circumstances. The *Directory for Masses with Children (DMC)* is such a document.

The *DMC* is written with pre-adolescent children in mind. It begins with a reiteration of the church's multi-faceted responsibility in the formation of children. But the bulk of the document outlines adaptations possible in celebrations in which children are in the majority. Many of its highlights have been discussed in the previous chapters. The remaining issues fall into the broader categories of ministries, participation and the parts of the mass.

Ministries

The Students

The *DMC* encourages a diversity of ministries and the participation of children in special ministries (#24 and #22). Experience has shown that this principle is subject to certain limitations. First, children chosen to exercise a special ministry must have the required abilities and training. Second, children must not be led to believe that, unless they have a special ministry, they have no role or ministry at all. In other words, the same principles apply to students as to adults: students should not be called to ministry simply because it's their turn or because they need or deserve public recognition. Liturgy is not the place for showcasing such individuals. With very young children, the best way to heighten participation is to keep both the group and the worship space small. This far more effectively reduces the child's feeling of anonymity than does assigning children to ministries in which they are uncomfortable and for which they are not equipped. In addition, the last sentence of paragraph 22 is of great importance, "The children should not be allowed to forget that all forms of participation reach their high point in eucharistic communion ..."

The Priest

Paragraph 23 discusses at length the priest's role in establishing a festive, familial and meditative atmosphere for celebration. It recommends the free use of introductory comments by the priest; however, he must carefully prepare these comments in advance to avoid turning these moments into lessons whose more appropriate context is the classroom.

Priests who find it difficult to preach to children are allowed to delegate this ministry to other adults (#24). Hopefully, in such situations teachers would work with the priest over time to enable him to reassume this very important ministry.

Adults as Fellow Worshippers

Paragraph 24 is quite emphatic about the role of adults as fellow worshippers, rather than monitors. Experience has shown that a deliberate program of liturgical formation of both students and teachers makes this a strong possibility. In addition, though, it is of utmost importance that all adults who are present participate fully in the singing, gestures, processions, rituals and silence along with all the children. This means the priest, the teachers, parents, any adult guests, as well as older students. If a gesture or song is too childish for some who are present, then it is too childish for this liturgy. If children perceive that an adult or older student is not participating, one or more of the following is likely to occur:

1. Children assume this part is not important.

2. Children assume participation in this part is optional.

3. Children assume this is performance, not communal worship.

4. Children assume that celebration is really for little kids.

Other Kinds of Participation

The *DMC* recognizes the importance of embodying prayer, and recommends doing so by singing and music (#30), gesture (#33), sensory stimuli (#35 and #36), and the alternation of activity with silence and stillness (#37). And paragraph 34 presents an especially good rationale and outline of possibilities for effective use of processions in celebrations with children. Sensory appeal in liturgy involves the rich use of signs which appeal to the sense of sight: large gestures by the priest and other ministers, highly visible ritual acts, colourful vesture and decor, special-looking materials (books, candles, dishes, cloths, etc.); and to the senses of taste and smell: liberal use of incense, real homemade bread, wine which is shared by all. Children should have ample opportunity to touch sacred things appropriately: to carry and venerate the book of God's word, to present the gifts for use in the liturgy of the eucharist, to help prepare the altar and wash the priest's hands.

Adaptations of the Parts of the Mass

While liturgy is certainly open to adaptation, liturgy planners must always remember that there are limits to adaptation. Paragraph 21 states unequivocally that "these eucharistic celebrations must lead children toward the celebrations of Mass with adults ... " To this end, paragraph 39 warns that some parts may never be adapted lest the difference between school and parish liturgy become counter-productive.

What major adaptations does the *DMC* recommend in the parts of the mass? In the introductory rites, the document recommends paring down the rites to make clear their preparatory nature, and it leaves the door open to the careful inclusion of elements to create the appropriate mood for celebration. For this reason, those wishing to present student work and other 'thematic' items in a procession should use them within the opening procession and not delay their inclusion until the procession with the gifts for the liturgy of the eucharist, where they would be inappropriate.

In the liturgy of the word, the *DMC* allows reducing the number and length of the biblical readings. The only reading required in celebrations with very young children is the gospel. Although use of the prescribed readings of the day is considered a strict mandate in most circumstances, the *DMC* allows other biblical readings to be substituted if prescribed readings are considered unsuitable for the children. Some examples of "unsuitable" readings include: a text which is too long and cannot be shortened without a loss of meaning, a text that details a single episode from a long Old Testament saga which the students will meet out of context, a text whose subject matter is inappropriate or incomprehensible to young children (e.g., fornication), a text which would require an inordinate amount of catechesis in preparation for its hearing. Although, in the selection of readings, the document insists that "Everything depends on the spiritual advantage that the reading can bring to the children," it also strictly forbids the use of paraphrases of scripture in place of genuine translations (#44).

Where do we turn if the readings of the day are "unsuitable"? Begin by consulting the readings of the other days in the same week, the surrounding Sundays, and other days in the liturgical season. Try the same days in the other years of the lectionaries. (The Sunday lectionary has three years, A, B and C; the weekday has I and II.) If these all prove unsuitable, the readings used in the current unit of the religion program may be useful, since the CCCB catechetical series is liturgically oriented. If all these prove unsuitable, perhaps this is not an appropriate occasion or 'theme' for liturgy. If you are still convinced that it is, try looking up a key word in a biblical concordance. (A biblical concordance lists in alphabetical order all the words used in the Bible and indicates where to find them.)

The *DMC* describes the liturgy of the word as the "reading and explanation" of the word. However, some enlightened nuancing of this vocabulary is in order. Paragraph 47 is particularly misleading in its recommendations. The strategies suggested are certainly valuable, but are more suited to the period of classroom preparation in advance of the celebration. Surely a didactic approach is not in harmony with the document's insistence on the festive, affective nature of the liturgy. In liturgical celebrations, the word is to be boldly proclaimed and celebrated, not merely read. And certainly the liturgy is no place for explaining scripture as at its first hearing. The explanation, which is rightly a part of the liturgy of the word, does not simply impart information, but invites and exhorts us to respond in celebration and mission in the world. (For a more complete presentation on this kind of explanation, see *Preparing to Preach* in this series.)

The *DMC* allows great adaptation of the prayers proclaimed by the priest according to the needs of the children, and appropriately cautions us against becoming moralistic or childish. Following the publication of the *DMC*, because free textual adaptation of the eucharistic prayer was not allowed, three eucharistic prayers were approved for use at masses with children; you will find them in the sacramentary. These special eucharistic prayers preserve the purpose and structure of the eucharistic prayer, but express its meaning in vocabulary more suited to children. They also allow more opportunities for children to be involved in the eucharistic prayer by means of acclamations. It is imperative that school liturgy planners become familiar with these prayers and plan a gradual course, perhaps covering two or three years, for introducing them to students.

In the concluding rites, the *DMC* asks that the dismissal make clear to the children the connection between liturgy and life. In a very few words, it should remind the children that the mystery celebrated calls them to a way of living and being in the world.

In Summary

1. The *DMC* outlines possibilities for adapting the liturgy when the majority in the assembly are children. Its ultimate goal is full, conscious and active participation of children in celebrations with the full community.

2. It must be clear to children that participation has many forms.

3. The liturgy exerts its formative power best when strong symbols and sensory stimuli are used. Liturgical celebrations must be festive, never didactic.

4. Well-prepared textual adaptations can make the celebration festive, familial and meditative for the children. (Three special eucharistic prayers have been written for use in masses with children.)

5. Adults attend as fellow worshippers and model full, conscious and active participation.

Discussion Questions

1. To what extent has your school made use of the *Directory for Masses with Children*?

2. How are liturgical ministers chosen and prepared for their special roles?

3. At what points in school celebrations are adults tempted to withdraw into the role of monitor? Discuss possible causes and solutions.

4. How much effort has gone into embodying prayer in school celebrations? What would you suggest might be done in preparing this year's liturgies to strengthen this dimension of your celebrations?

5. The eucharistic prayers for masses with children are relatively unfamiliar to many, including many priests. Examine the prayers and discuss which you will introduce to the students this year.

Especially for teachers

1. How do you involve the priest in your preparations?

2. How and when is the priest informed of your plans and the extent of your preparations?

3. Have you discussed the state of school liturgies with your pastor?

Especially for presiders

1. What do you do personally to ensure that celebrations are festive?

2. Do you prepare your comments in advance?

3. Have you enlisted the assistance of teachers in preparing for your role in school celebrations?

4. Do your homilies give the children a reason to join in the praise of God with joy and enthusiasm?

5. How familiar are you with the three eucharistic prayers for masses with children?

Where Do We Go From Here?

(or Does That Make It a Beginning?)

At the outset I promised to tackle your liturgical problems at their source. To this end I invited you to list the problems and joys you are currently encountering in your school celebrations. I hope you noted, as you progressed through the book, which parts of the book addressed your particular problems and which affirmed your joys. Now you ask: Where do we go from here?

Since the question of "Why" came first in the book, it would be a fruitful exercise to compose a statement about the "why" of celebration in your particular situation. Hint: it should include something about paschal mystery and something about liturgical formation and participation in celebrations with adults.

With a clear statement of purpose in hand, it will be much easier to draw up a realistic long-range action plan. Begin by establishing a celebration schedule (see Chapters 1 and 3) including eucharist, word, morning or evening prayer, reconciliation and devotions as well as rehearsal time for each as needed. This will help clarify the time-line for your action plan. Include in your plan items of ritual vocabulary (see Chapter 2) that will receive attention in the preparations and in the celebration itself. Map out the development of your school's repertoire of liturgical music (see Chapter 5) and add this to your schedule as well. Designate a suitable space for each celebration and specify how the space will be used, adapted, marked, decorated, etc. (see Chapter 4).

Well in advance of each celebration, sit down with the presider, the texts, the *DMC* and your formation goals to work out details (see Chapter 6), to script textual changes, introductory remarks and other comments, and to share insights for the construction of a homily which will lift children's hearts for the praise of God.

And don't forget to sit down soon after the event to evaluate and make any necessary revisions to your action plan. A written record of your plan, of each event and of your evaluations will be most helpful to keep the program on track and moving.

Liturgical formation requires work. But if we consider the intimate link between our children's faith-life and the quality of our celebrations, we can't afford not to do it.

GLOSSARY

Celebration: Even when used in a liturgical or religious context, the term denotes a festive event characterized by joyous, enthusiastic singing and eager participation in all activities by all in attendance.

Celebration of the word: festive occasion celebrating the good news and honouring Christ who is present and speaks in the word proclaimed. It has the same format as the liturgy of the word at mass: readings, responsorial psalm, gospel acclamation and procession, homily, profession of faith and general intercessions. It should include joyful songs of praise and other sensually appealing indicators of our esteem for God's word: incense, candles, processions, gestures of honour.

Devotions: ritual practices which the church recognizes as helpful for the spiritual life of Christians, but does not consider part of its universal and official worship.

Eucharist: Derived from the Greek word for thanksgiving, eucharist refers to the church's main liturgical action in the Sunday assembly. Use of this term for the action of the assembly indicates that the heart of the liturgy is our praise and thanks of God, through, with and in Christ, by the power of the Holy Spirit.

Eucharistic prayer: prayer which is the heart of the mass, whose proclamation makes the celebration a celebration of the eucharist. It begins with the ancient dialogue which includes the command: "Lift up your hearts." It ends with the Amen of the great doxology, "Through him, with him and in him, in the unity of the Holy Spirit, all glory and honour are yours, almighty Father, for ever and ever."

Liturgical year: The church celebrates the paschal mystery in cycles and seasons. The seasons of special festivity are Advent, the Christmas season (which extends to the feast of the Baptism of the Lord), Lent, the paschal Triduum and the Easter season (which extends to Pentecost). The rest of the year is called Ordinary Time and the Sundays of Ordinary Time are referred to by number. Devotional months (May and October for Mary, June for the Sacred Heart) are not part of the liturgical year.

Liturgy: Liturgy encompasses all the official worship of the church: celebrations of the eucharist and the other sacraments, the liturgy of the hours, and the liturgical year.

Morning and evening prayer: In obedience to the biblical admonition to rejoice always and pray constantly, the church designates certain hours of the day as official times of prayer. Hence the formal name 'liturgy of the hours.' The most important of these hours are morning and evening. At each of these hours the church exercises the priestly office of Christ by offering praise (using the texts of the psalms) and petition to God on behalf of the world. A proclamation of scripture may also be included.

Mass: This is another name for the celebration of eucharist. It is an example of naming the whole after one of its parts. It comes from *missa*, the Latin term used to designate the dismissal at the end of celebration, "Go in peace to love and serve the Lord." When fully understood, use of this term emphasizes the missionary thrust of the eucharist.

Paraliturgy: There is no such thing. The word you want is 'celebration.'

Paschal mystery: "Paschal" is derived from *pasch*, meaning *passover*. In Christian usage the word "paschal" refers to the passover of Christ: his gift of himself in life and death, his passage through death to new life and Spirit-filled glory. It also encompasses the mystery of our salvation by our passage in baptism into Christ's new, glorified life.

Preface: The preface is the technical name of the part of the eucharistic prayer between the "Lift up your hearts" dialogue and the "Holy, holy."

Ritual: Any patterned behaviour is rightly called a ritual. In religious contexts it usually involves the use of objects and gestures with special meaning.

BIBLIOGRAPHY

Recommended Reading

Born of the Spirit Series. Ottawa: Canadian Conference of Catholic Bishops. A Canadian catechetical program for children from Early Childhood level to grade six. Each year of the program is developed in light of the liturgical year and includes several well-designed celebrations.

Children's Daily Prayer. Chicago: Liturgy Training Publications. A very good adaptation of the liturgy of the hours for use in schools. Musical settings for the psalms would make it even better. Published annually.

Marian Year 1987-1988. Ottawa: CCCB. 1987. A user-friendly guide to celebrating Mary. Excellent background information, as well as outlines for celebrations.

The Liturgy Documents: A Parish Resource. 3rd edition. Chicago: Liturgy Training Publications. 1991. A collection of 12 important liturgical documents, with commentary. Includes: Constitution on the Sacred Liturgy, Directory for Masses with Children and Music in Catholic Worship. Some are documents of the universal church; some are American, but all contain sound liturgical principles honoured by prominent liturgists world-wide.

Documents on the Liturgy: 1963-1979. Conciliar, Papal, Curial Texts. Collegeville, MN: The Liturgical Press, 1983. This vast reference work contains 554 official documents of the church issued from the time of Vatican II up to 1979.

Celebrating School Liturgies: Guidelines for Planning. Joan Vos. Collegeville: MN: The Liturgical Press, 1991. Recognizing that teachers often have all too little time to help students prepare liturgies, this book provides a step-by-step guide to that process.

MEMBER OF SCABRINI MEDIA

Quebec, Canada
2002